Food Around the World

Robert Quinn

Contents

OXFORD
UNIVERSITY PRESS

OXFORD
UNIVERSITY PRESS

Great Clarendon Street, Oxford OX2 6DP

Oxford University Press is a department of the University of Oxford. It furthers the University's objective of excellence in research, scholarship, and education by publishing worldwide in

Oxford New York

Auckland Cape Town Dar es Salaam Hong Kong Karachi Kuala Lumpur Madrid Melbourne Mexico City Nairobi New Delhi Shanghai Taipei Toronto

With offices in

Argentina Austria Brazil Chile Czech Republic France Greece Guatemala Hungary Italy Japan Poland Portugal Singapore South Korea Switzerland Thailand Turkey Ukraine Vietnam

OXFORD and OXFORD ENGLISH are registered trade marks of Oxford University Press in the UK and in certain other countries

© Oxford University Press 2010

The moral rights of the author have been asserted

Database right Oxford University Press (maker)

First published 2010
2018
18

ISBN: 978 0 19 464557 7

An Audio Pack containing this book and an Audio download is also available ISBN: 978 0 19 402245 3

This book is also available as an e-Book,
ISBN: 978 0 19 410914 7

An accompanying Activity Book is also available
ISBN: 978 0 19 464567 6

Printed in China

This book is printed on paper from certified and well-managed sources.

ACKNOWLEDGEMENTS

Illustrations by: Alan Rowe pp 36, 44, 50, 52, 53; Gary Swift pp5, 9, 22, 29, 34.

The publisher would like to thank the following for their kind permission to reproduce photographs and other copyright material: Alamy pp3, 17 (rice on tray/Pixmann Ltd), 7 (olive oil/foodfolio) 10 (chickens/Paddy McGuinness), 11 (fishermen/MIXA Co., Ltd.), 14 (Old ice cream maker/Foodcollection.com), 16 (star shaped pasta/imagebroker), 17 (kimchi pots/Photosynthesis), 18 (making tortillas/Robert Fried), 21 (horchata/Emilio Ereza), 23 (tamarind cocktail/Bon Appetit), 24 (street food vendor/Andre Seale), 25 (street food vendor/David Noton Photography), 27 (simit seller/Oleg Boldyrev), 27 (Kebab shop/Robert Harding Picture Library Ltd), 30 (maple syrup forest/icpix_can), 34 (yam market/Danita Delimont), 35 (Sikh festival/Richard Levine), 26 (fries/Steven Mark Needham/Envision), 26 (eating waffles/Mika/zefa), 32 (thanksgiving dinner/moodboard); Getty pp3, 28 (trifle/Dorling Kindersley), 3, 19 (tagine/Foodcollection), 4 (carbohydrates/Dorling Kindersley), 5 (proteins/Dorling Kindersley), 7 (glass of milk/Photographer's Choice/Michael Rosenfeld), 7 (beef on bbq/Hola Images), 8 (arable farmer/Medioimages/Photodisc), 9 (paddy fields/Gallo Images/Travel Ink), 12 (corn/Foodcollection), 13 (picking chocolate/AFP), 15 (fries/Sisse Brimberg & Cotton Coulson, Keenpress/National Geographic), 20 (lassi drink/Dorling Kindersley); Grapheast p22 (baobab drink from Africa/Stock Food/Aline Princet); iStockPhotos pp3, 16 (pizza/Konstantin Papadakis), 7 (nuts/Marcelo Wain), p7 (fruit/fajean), p7 (spinach/christine Balderas), 9 (kiwi fruit/Suzannah Skelton), 10 (farmyard/Gene Krebs), 14 (ice cream/christopher Conrad), 15 (potatoes/John Steele), pp15 (crisps/creacart), 21 (cinnamon stick/Alina Solovyova-Vincent), 29 (durian fruit/Yong Hian Lim), 30 (maple syrup bottle/Valerie Loiseleux), 31 (purple corn/Mehmet Salih Guler), Lacuma Society pp3, 31 (lacuma); Reuters p35 (famine); Susi Paz p29 (alpokat drink); Yonhap Korean News Agency p33 (chuseok festivities/Yonhap).

Introduction

Everyone needs to eat food. Farmers grow fruits, vegetables, rice, and wheat for people to eat. They also raise animals for meat and milk. People around the world eat lots of different food. Different countries have different typical dishes.

What are the typical dishes in your country?
What are your favorite dishes?
What are the names of the foods below?
Where in the world are they popular?

Now read and discover more about food around the world!

Everyone needs food to live. It gives you energy to work and play. It also gives you nutrients to grow well and stay healthy. Do you eat a balanced diet with lots of different nutrients?

Proteins

Your body needs proteins to build muscles. Proteins are also important for healthy hair and fingernails. You can get lots of proteins from meat, fish, and eggs. Dairy products, like milk, cheese, and yogurt, also contain proteins. Many people don't eat animal products, but they can get proteins from plant products. Pulses, like beans and lentils, are rich in proteins. Many grains, nuts, and seeds have proteins, too. Which of these foods do you eat?

Carbohydrates

Carbohydrates give your body energy. You can get carbohydrates from grain products like rice, bread, and pasta. Your body digests these foods slowly, so they give you energy for many hours. Some vegetables, like potatoes, also have lots of carbohydrates. What grains and vegetables do you eat?

Sugar is also a carbohydrate. Your body digests sugar quickly, so it gives you energy right away. Don't eat too many sweet foods like candy or ice cream, and remember that you can also get sugar from naturally sweet foods. Have a bowl of fruit with a little honey!

Discover!

We also need to drink lots of water to stay healthy. Did you know that about 70% of your body is water?

Fats

You need to eat some fats to grow well and stay healthy. Your body also stores fats for extra energy, and to keep you warm in winter. Some types of meat and fish have a lot of fats. Dairy products, like butter and cheese, have fats, too. You can also get fats from plant products like nuts, seeds, and vegetable oils. Be careful – too many fats can make you fat!

Vitamins

Your body needs vitamins to stay healthy and fight diseases. Vitamin A keeps your skin healthy. You can get vitamin A from orange fruits and vegetables like carrots or pumpkins. Dark green vegetables, like spinach, have lots of vitamin A, too. Dairy products give you vitamin B for healthy blood. You can also get vitamin B from meat, fish, and eggs. Vitamin C helps your body fight diseases. You can get vitamin C from citrus fruits like oranges and lemons.

Minerals

Your body also needs minerals. You need calcium for strong bones and healthy teeth. Dairy products, like milk and yogurt, are good sources of calcium. You also need iron for healthy blood. You can get iron from red meat and eggs, or from vegetables like broccoli and spinach. Salt is also an important mineral, but be careful! Too much salty food is bad for you.

Go to pages 36–37 for activities.

2 Food Producers

Do you know where rice comes from? Where do we get our fruits and vegetables? And who produces the milk that we drink or the seafood that we eat?

Arable Farmers

Arable farmers grow crops that we can eat. Some crops, like rice, wheat, and vegetables, grow in fields. Before farmers plant their crops, they plow their fields. Some farmers use animals, like horses or oxen, to help. Other farmers use modern machines. Then farmers sow seeds or plant seedlings. When the crops are ready, the farmers harvest them and take them to markets.

Some fruits, like melons, are grown in fields. Other fruits, like apples, cherries, or kiwi fruits, are grown on trees in orchards. Sometimes farmers harvest the fruits with machines, but some fruits, like peaches, are very delicate. Farmers have to pick them by hand. That's very hard work!

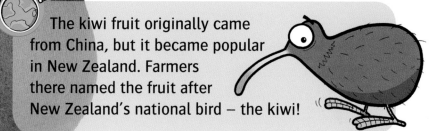

Discover!

The kiwi fruit originally came from China, but it became popular in New Zealand. Farmers there named the fruit after New Zealand's national bird – the kiwi!

Plants need water to grow and produce crops. In some parts of the world it doesn't rain much, so farmers use irrigation systems to water their plants. Rice plants need lots of water, so farmers grow them in wet fields called paddy fields. The paddy fields are often in flat areas near rivers. In some countries, like Vietnam, farmers build terraces of paddy fields on the sides of hills to grow as much rice as possible.

Paddy Fields, Vietnam

Livestock Farmers

Livestock farmers raise animals, like cows and sheep, to produce food. These animals give us meat, and dairy products like milk, cheese, and butter. The animals often live in open pastures where they eat grass and other plants. Some farmers have to travel long distances with their animals to find green pastures.

Some farm animals, like chickens, are raised in closed yards. This keeps them together and protects them. Farmers sometimes build houses called coops where the chickens can sleep and lay their eggs.

Fishermen

Some fishermen catch fish, like trout, in lakes and rivers. Other fishermen work at sea where they catch saltwater fish like tuna or cod. They also catch seafood like prawns or squid. Some fishermen work far from the coast on deep-sea fishing boats. They often use very big nets. Deep-sea fishing boats also have freezers to keep the fish cold until the fishermen return to the port.

Some fish are raised on fish farms. The fish live in artificial ponds or in closed areas on the coast. This fishing industry is called aquaculture. Some types of shellfish, like oysters, are also raised this way.

Discover!

Tsukiji Market in Tokyo in Japan is the largest fish market in the world. It sells about 2,000 metric tons of fish and seafood every day!

Go to pages 38–39 for activities.

Some of our favorite foods have a long history. Did you know that popcorn is thousands of years old? Do you know who invented potato chips, or where chocolate was discovered?

Popcorn

People started growing corn for food about 8,000 years ago in Central America. They used the corn in many ways. They ate it fresh and they used it to make bread and soups. Did you know that they also invented popcorn? In 1948 archaeologists found popcorn in a cave. It was about 5,500 years old!

Native Americans made popcorn by cooking the corn over a fire. People enjoyed eating the hot popcorn. They also used it to make decorations and popcorn necklaces!

Chocolate

The native people of Central America also invented chocolate about 2,000 years ago. They made a spicy drink from the seeds of the cacao tree. First they dried the cacao seeds and crushed them to make a paste. Then they added chili peppers and water. The chocolate drink wasn't sweet – it was bitter!

Spanish explorers learned about chocolate when they arrived in America, and it soon became a popular drink in Spain. Spanish people liked their chocolate hot, with sugar and cinnamon. Hot chocolate later became popular all over Europe, and chocolate factories started making chocolate candy, too. In 1867 a Swiss chocolate maker named Daniel Peter invented a chocolate candy made with milk. Now milk chocolate is very popular, and cacao trees are grown in many places.

Cacao Trees, Africa

Ice Cream

About 2,000 years ago the Ancient Romans brought ice and snow from the mountains and mixed it with fruit and honey. About 1,500 years ago people in China made desserts with ice and milk. The soft ice cream that we eat today was probably invented in Europe about 400 years ago.

Fruit ices were popular in Europe. Then people started to add cream. They put the cream in a metal bowl with sugar. Then they froze it in a bucket of ice. This was hard work because they had to keep mixing the cream by hand. In 1843 an American woman named Nancy Johnson invented an ice cream machine. Seven years later the first ice cream factory opened in Baltimore in the USA.

An Ice Cream Machine

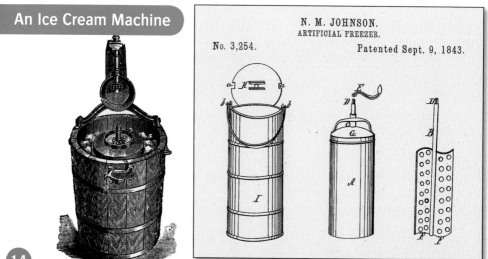

N. M. JOHNSON.
ARTIFICIAL FREEZER.

No. 3,254.

Patented Sept. 9, 1843.

Potato Chips

In 1853 George Crum was a cook in a restaurant in Saratoga Springs in New York. One day, a customer said he didn't like George's French fries. He said they were too thick! So George played a joke on the customer. He made some French fries that were very thin, like paper. The customer loved them!

Soon all of George's customers wanted thin French fries. George called them Saratoga chips. In 1860 George opened a new restaurant and his thin chips became famous all over the USA. Today potato chips are one of the most popular snacks in the world.

Discover!

In the United Kingdom, French fries are called chips, and potato chips are called crisps!

Go to pages 40–41 for activities.

4 Typical Dishes

Every country has typical dishes that are popular with local people. These dishes are often made in a traditional way, with special ingredients. What types of dishes are typical in your country?

Italy

Pasta is the most typical food in Italy. Italian pasta is made from wheat flour and comes in many different shapes. For example, spaghetti is long and straight, *spirali* pasta is a spiral shape, and *stellini* pasta is a star shape. What type of pasta do you prefer?

Pizza is another typical dish in Italy. Italian pizza is usually made with wheat flour, tomato, and mozzarella cheese. Some people also add meat, seafood, or vegetables. Most pizzas are round, but in Rome they also make special square pizzas!

Rice is a very important Korean food, and most Koreans eat some rice every day. They often eat rice with dishes of meat, seafood, and vegetables. Koreans also use rice to make soup, rice cakes, and a sweet dessert drink called *sikhye*.

Do you like spicy food? You should try some Korean *kimchi*. It's a spicy dish made with cabbage, onions, garlic, chili peppers, and salt. Many people have their own special recipe. Most Koreans eat some *kimchi* every day. It's a very healthy food because it has lots of vitamins.

Discover!

Traditional *kimchi* is made in pottery jars. People put the jars underground to keep the *kimchi* at exactly the right temperature.

Mexico

Mexican tortillas are a type of thin, flat bread. They are usually made with corn flour, but some people use wheat flour. First you cook them in a hot pan. Then you fill them with meat, cheese, beans, and vegetables. Mexican tortillas are soft, so you can fold them to keep the food inside. You can also eat them with your fingers!

Mole poblano is another typical dish in Mexico. It's a thick sauce made with chili peppers, nuts, seeds, and spices. Chocolate is also a secret ingredient! Mexicans use *mole poblano* to make lots of dishes. The most popular dish is made with turkey. It's a Mexican national dish.

Morocco

Couscous is one of the most typical foods in Morocco. It's made from wheat. The couscous grains are small when they are dry. Then they get bigger when they are cooked with water. Moroccans often eat couscous with meat and vegetable dishes. They also use it to make cool summer salads or sweet dessert cakes.

Another typical food in Morocco is *tajine*. It's a hot dish made with vegetables and meat or seafood. People also add nuts and dried fruit like raisins. They cook the *tajine* very slowly in a *tajine* pot. When it's ready, they serve it with couscous or fresh bread. It's delicious!

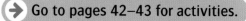 Go to pages 42–43 for activities.

 # 5 Cool Drinks

What do you like to drink when the weather is hot? Everybody needs to drink water, but there are lots of other cool drinks. People often drink fruit juice or soda, but in some countries they prefer other types of drink. Some of these drinks are quite unusual!

India

Lassi is a popular Indian drink. It's made with yogurt, and it can be sweet or savory. Many people drink it in summer, but some people like to drink it all year long. To make sweet *lassi*, you mix some yogurt, sugar, and ice with a blender. You can add fresh fruit like mangos, bananas, or strawberries. To make savory *lassi*, you mix the yogurt with salt. Some people also like to add pepper and other spices. Which type of *lassi* would you like to try?

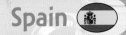

Horchata is a traditional drink in some parts of Spain. It looks like a vanilla milkshake, but it isn't made with milk – it's made with tiger nuts! They are pulses that grow underground.

To make *horchata*, you leave the tiger nuts in water for a day. Then you squeeze the juice out of them. You can add sugar, lemon, and cinnamon. *Horchata* is also the name of a drink in Mexico, but it tastes very different. It's made with rice!

Discover!

Cinnamon is a spice. It comes from the bark of cinnamon trees. Many people use cinnamon in sweet dishes, but it's also good in savory dishes.

Sudan

Gubdi is a special drink from Sudan. It's made from the fruit of the baobab tree. Farmers like to drink it in the summer because it's very refreshing. Baobab fruit is also called monkey's bread! It's very healthy because it contains lots of carbohydrates and proteins. It also has more vitamin C than oranges!

To make *gubdi*, you break open the baobab fruit and take out the dry pulp. Then you put the pulp in water and squeeze it to make a white juice. Some people also use baobab fruit to make ice cream and milkshakes.

Discover!

The baobab tree is also called the upside-down tree. Can you see why?

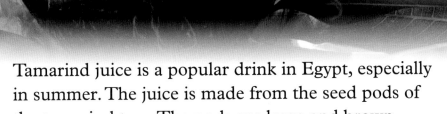

Tamarind juice is a popular drink in Egypt, especially in summer. The juice is made from the seed pods of the tamarind tree. The pods are large and brown. People also just eat them fresh.

To make tamarind juice, you put the pods in water for two or three hours. Then you take out the pulp and cook it in hot water. After that you take out the seeds. Finally you add cold water, ice, and spices. Tamarind juice is sour, so most people also add sugar.

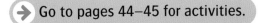 Go to pages 44–45 for activities.

23

6 Street Food

Many people like eating in the street. They can eat quickly and the food is usually cheap. There are lots of different street foods around the world. What are the most popular street foods in your country?

Brazil

One of the most typical street foods in Brazil is *pão de queijo*. It's a ball of warm bread made with tapioca flour and cheese. Some street vendors also sell barbecued chicken or spicy prawns. If you're thirsty, try some *acai*. It's a popular drink made from palm tree berries. For dessert you can have fresh fruit or you can try some sweet coconut pastries. If you want a snack later, you can have popcorn with sugar. It's a popular snack all over Brazil.

Thailand

Street food is very popular in Thailand. There are lots of food stalls and carts, and you can also see vendors on bicycles, motorcycles, or boats! Some of the most typical street foods are spicy Thai noodles and sticky rice with peanuts. If you like meat you can also have some satays. They are pieces of meat that people barbecue on sticks. If you like fish, why not try some fried fishcakes? You can watch the vendor fry them right in front of you. Later you can have some mango for dessert. It's very sweet!

Discover! Sticky rice is easy to eat with chopsticks because the grains of rice stick together!

Belgium

French fries are one of the most popular street foods in Belgium. In Belgium they are called *friet*. You can buy French fries from stalls or carts in many streets and public squares. Belgian people like to add sauces to their French fries, like mayonnaise, ketchup, or curry sauce. Some people like to mix different sauces and add other ingredients, like onions or meat.

Then you can buy a Belgian waffle for dessert. You can also put some ice cream on top, with chocolate, fruit, or cream. Yummy!

At breakfast time many Turkish people eat a special bread called *simit*. It's a bread ring with sesame seeds on top. You can buy *simit* rings from street carts. For lunch, you can have a doner kebab. A doner kebab is thin pieces of meat that you can eat with flat bread. You can also add some salad.

Another popular street food is corn that's cooked in water. You can buy it from street carts, and in the summer you can buy it at the beach, too. If you're thirsty, why not try some *visne* juice? It's a sweet drink that's made from sour cherries.

What street food would you like to try?

→ Go to pages 46–47 for activities.

27

Special Desserts

Do you have a sweet tooth? There are lots of desserts that you can try from around the world. Do you like pastries and cakes, or do you prefer milkshakes and ice cream? What's the best dessert from your country?

The United Kingdom

Custard is a traditional British dessert. It's a creamy pudding made with eggs, milk, sugar, and vanilla. To make custard, you mix all the ingredients and then cook them very slowly. You can eat the custard warm or cold. Some British people like to put custard on other desserts like fruit pies.

Custard is also used to make fruit trifle. Trifle is a traditional British dessert made with cake, custard, fruit, and jelly. Jelly is fruit gelatine. Most people also put lots of cream on top. It's a very rich dessert!

Indonesia

Alpokat is a special milkshake from Indonesia. It's made with avocado! First you use a blender to mix the avocado pulp with milk. Then you pour it into a glass and add chocolate milk. It's unusual, but it's very good!

Durian fruit is a popular dessert in Indonesia. Durians are a spiky fruit with a very sweet, creamy pulp. They also have a very strong smell. Some people say durians smell terrible, but other people love them. If you want to try some durian you can eat it fresh or you can have some durian ice cream. You might like it!

Discover!

In some parts of Indonesia you can't eat durian fruit on public transportation. Some people don't like the strong smell!

Canada 🍁

Maple syrup is traditional in Canada. It's made from the sap of maple trees. You can see a red maple leaf on Canada's national flag. The maple sap is collected in early spring. People cut small holes in the sides of the trees and collect the sap in buckets. Then they cook the sap to take out the water and make syrup. If they continue cooking the sap, it turns into maple candy. A lot of Canadians put maple syrup on their pancakes. They also add it to cakes, cookies, and other desserts.

Discover!

All trees have sap inside them. It takes 40 liters of maple tree sap to make a liter of pure maple syrup.

In Peru, people eat a traditional dessert called *mazamorra morada*. This dessert is dark purple because it's made from purple corn! Peruvians cook the corn with sugar, spices, and fruit like green apples and pineapple. Then they mix it with dried fruits.

Another dessert in Peru is *lucuma* fruit. It's a tropical fruit that is green on the outside and orange on the inside. Some people say *lucuma* fruit has a sweet, nutty flavor. They often use it to make desserts like ice cream, milkshakes, pastries, and cakes.

Lucuma Fruit

→ Go to pages 48–49 for activities.

  Giving Thanks

People work hard for the food that we have and not everyone has enough food. There are many harvest festivals around the world when farmers and other people give thanks for the food that they have harvested. Are there any harvest festivals in your country?

The United States of America

In the USA, people celebrate a festival called Thanksgiving Day on the fourth Thursday of November. Families usually get together for a big holiday meal. The most typical foods are turkey with potatoes and seasonal vegetables. Many people also have some cranberry sauce with their turkey. The most popular desserts are pumpkin pie or apple pie with ice cream. On Thanksgiving Day, many people also like to watch American football on television. It's a tradition!

Ghana

In Ghana, people celebrate the *Homowo* festival in late August or early September, at the beginning of the harvest season. Yams are one of the main crops in Ghana, so a good harvest is important. To celebrate the festival, people dig up fresh yams from the fields. They give the best yams to their ancestors to give thanks for the harvest. After that they have a big meal. They prepare lots of dishes with yams and other seasonal vegetables like corn and beans. During the festival, people wear bright clothes and there is lots of singing and dancing.

Discover!

Yams can be very big. Some yams are more than 2 meters long and can weigh more than 60 kilograms!

Korea

In September or October, Koreans celebrate a harvest festival called *Chuseok*. It's also a day for people to remember their ancestors. In the morning, people go to the cemetery to visit their family tombs. They clean the tombs and they leave food and other gifts to show respect. Many Koreans travel long distances to be with their families on this special day.

The most traditional food for *Chuseok* is a rice cake called *songpyeon*. The cakes are usually filled with beans, but some people also use sesame seeds. People like to play traditional games and some women also do a special circle dance.

Making *Songpyeon*, Korea

In India, many people celebrate *Baisakhi*. This festival is at the beginning of the harvest season in April. In the morning, people visit temples to give thanks for the harvest. Then they go home to prepare a family meal. Some popular festival foods are cold salads with lentils or potatoes, and hot curry dishes with vegetables or meat. Most people eat these dishes with rice and flat bread. For dessert they often eat sweet cakes made with sesame seeds and spices. In many parts of India there are also big street parades.

Discover!

Be thankful for food! Millions of children around the world don't have enough to eat. The United Nations Children's Fund (UNICEF) works to help these children and their families.

→ Go to pages 50–51 for activities.

1 Food for Life

← Read pages 4–7.

1 Complete the sentences.

diseases ~~energy~~ calcium muscles oils

1 Carbohydrates give us _____energy_____ to work and play.

2 Our bodies use proteins to build _____.

3 We can get some fats from vegetable _____.

4 Vitamins help our bodies to fight _____.

5 Our bodies need minerals like _____ and iron.

2 Answer the questions.

1 What does rice give us? _Rice gives us carbohydrates._

2 What do eggs give us? _____

3 What do oranges give us? _____

4 What does broccoli give us? _____

5 What do carrots give us? _____

6 What does honey give us? _____

3 **Match.**

1 We can get sugar   our skin healthy.

2 Our bodies store   to grow healthy hair.

3 We need proteins   can be bad for our health.

4 Vitamin A keeps   from naturally sweet foods.

5 Our bodies need iron   for healthy blood.

6 Too much salt   fats for extra energy.

4 **Answer the questions.**

1 Why does sugar give us energy right away?

_____

2 What plant products can give us proteins?

_____

3 What nutrients do we get from nuts and seeds?

_____

4 Why do our bodies need vitamin C to stay healthy?

_____

5 What vitamin can we get from meat and fish?

_____

6 What foods are good sources of calcium?

_____

5 **Write about your diet. What foods do you eat?**

_____

_____

_____

2 Food Producers

← Read pages 8–11.

1 Complete the chart.

dairy products ~~wheat~~ tuna cherries trout
prawns vegetables meat eggs

Arable Farmers	Livestock Farmers	Fishermen
wheat		

2 Write sentences.

~~Arable farmers~~ raise animals. Fruit is grown ~~grow crops.~~
Livestock farmers in fields and orchards. catch seafood.
Some fishermen need lots of water. Some plants

1 _Arable farmers grow crops._

2 _____

3 _____

4 _____

5 _____

3 Circle the correct words.

1 Farmers need to **grow** / **plow** their fields.

2 Delicate fruit is often picked by **hand** / **machine**.

3 Cows are often raised in **pastures** / **orchards**.

4 Rice is grown in wet fields called **coops** / **paddy fields**.

5 Some types of fish, like trout, live in **rivers** / **seas**.

6 Some fish are raised on **fish farms** / **fishing boats**.

4 Answer the questions.

1 Where are wheat and vegetables grown?

_____

2 What crops are grown on trees in orchards?

_____

3 What animals produce dairy products?

_____

4 Why are some farm animals raised in closed yards?

_____

5 How do fishing boats keep the fish cold?

_____

5 Write the opposites. Find the page.

page

1 **dry** fields _____wet fields_____ _____

2 **natural** ponds _____ _____

3 **traditional** machines _____ _____

4 **freshwater** fish _____ _____

5 **hilly** areas _____ _____

3 Food Origins

← Read pages 12–15.

1 **Circle the correct words.**

1 The Ancient Romans made **potato chips** / **iced desserts**.

2 Popcorn originally came from **America** / **Europe**.

3 The first ice cream factory opened in **1850** / **1950**.

4 The world's first chocolate drink was **bitter** / **sweet**.

5 Saratoga chips were **thinner** / **fatter** than French fries.

2 **Match. Then complete the sentences.**

1843	popcorn
1853	potato chips
1948	ice cream
1867	milk chocolate

1 In _____ Nancy Johnson invented an _____ machine.

2 In _____ archaeologists found some very old _____ in a cave.

3 In _____ Daniel Peter invented _____ candy.

4 In _____ George Crum made some thin _____ .

3 **Order the words. Then write _true_ or _false_.**

1 in / was invented / Chocolate / China.

<u>Chocolate was invented in China.</u>   <u>false</u>

2 America. / popcorn / was made / The world's first / in

_____   _____

3 was invented / Central America. / Modern ice cream / in

_____   _____

4 popular / Spain. / Hot chocolate / very / in / became

_____   _____

5 Baltimore. / were invented / in / potato chips / Thin

_____   _____

4 **Answer the questions.**

1 Where did the Ancient Romans bring ice and snow from?

_____

2 Why didn't the customer like George's French fries?

_____

3 How did the Native Americans cook popcorn?

_____

4 Why was it hard work for people to make ice cream?

_____

5 What did the Native Americans add to the cacao paste?

_____

4 Typical Dishes

← Read pages 16–19.

1 Complete the chart. Then write sentences.

> couscous   pasta   *kimchi*   tortilla   rice
> *mole poblano*   ~~tajine~~   pizza

1 Morocco	2 Italy	3 Korea	4 Mexico
tajine			

1 <u>Couscous and tajine are typical foods in Morocco.</u>

2 _____

3 _____

4 _____

2 Write *true* or *false*.

1 Italian pizza is made with corn flour.   _____

2 *Mole poblano* is made with chocolate.   _____

3 *Sikhye* is a Mexican dish made from rice.   _____

4 Moroccan couscous is made from wheat.   _____

5 Korean *kimchi* has lots of vitamins.   _____

6 *Stellini* pasta is long and straight.   _____

3 Answer the questions.

1 How are Mexican tortillas cooked?

_____

2 What shape is *stellini* pasta?

_____

3 How often do most Koreans eat *kimchi*?

_____

4 What do Moroccans eat *tajine* with?

_____

5 Why can you fold Mexican tortillas?

_____

4 Complete the sentences.

> hot   flat   thick   sweet   spiral   spicy

1 *Mole poblano* is a _____ sauce.

2 *Kimchi* is a _____ vegetable dish.

3 *Spirali* pasta is a _____ shape.

4 Mexican tortillas are thin and _____ .

5 *Tajine* is a _____ Moroccan dish.

6 *Sikhye* is a _____ dessert drink.

5 Write about the typical dishes in your country.

_____

_____

_____

5 Cool Drinks

← Read pages 20–23.

1 Write the words.

> seed pods   baobab fruit   ice   tiger nuts   sugar   yogurt

1 _____

2 _____

3 _____

4 _____

5 _____

6 _____

2 Complete the sentences.

> fruit   juice   Indian   *horchata*   drink
> yogurt   seed pods   nuts

1 Spanish _____ is made with tiger _____.

2 Tamarind _____ is made from tamarind _____.

3 *Gubdi* is a _____ made from baobab _____.

4 *Lassi* is an _____ drink made with _____.

3 **Match. Then write the sentences.**

Sweet *lassi*	can be quite sour.
Mexican *horchata*	has sugar in it.
Baobab fruit	are large and brown.
Tamarind seed pods	cinnamon to *horchata*.
Some people add	is made with rice.
Tamarind juice	is also called monkey's bread.

1 _____

2 _____

3 _____

4 _____

5 _____

6 _____

4 **Answer the questions.**

1 When is *lassi* most popular?

_____

2 Where does cinnamon come from?

_____

3 Why do farmers in Sudan drink *gubdi*?

_____

4 Where do people drink tamarind juice?

_____

5 Where do tiger nuts grow?

_____

6 Street Food

← Read pages 24–27.

1 Match.

1 *pão de queijo*	Thai	palm berry juice
2 *visne* juice	Brazilian	cheese bread
3 *friet*	Belgian	barbecued meat
4 *acai*	Brazilian	a cherry drink
5 satays	Turkish	French fries

2 Answer the questions.

1 What is *pão de queijo*? _____

2 What is *visne* juice? _____

3 What are *friet*? _____

4 What is *acai*? _____

5 What are satays? _____

3 Complete the sentences.

sauces   dessert   sugar   bread   boats

1 In Brazil you can eat popcorn with _____.

2 Some vendors in Thailand work on _____.

3 Belgians put _____ on their French fries.

4 *Simit* rings are a type of Turkish _____.

5 You can have a Belgian waffle for _____.

4 **Order the words. Then answer the questions.**

1 have / you / What / can / for dessert / Brazil? / in

_____

_____

2 vendors / fried fishcakes? / Where / sell / do / Thai

_____

_____

3 do / put on / What / their waffles? / Belgian people

_____

_____

4 *simit* / buy / rings? / can / Where / you

_____

_____

5 sticky rice? / What / put on / Thai people / do

_____

_____

5 **Write about street food in your country.**

_____

_____

_____

_____

_____

7 Special Desserts

← Read pages 28–31.

1 Write the words.

> avocado milkshake   *lucuma* fruit   custard
> maple syrup   trifle   durian fruit

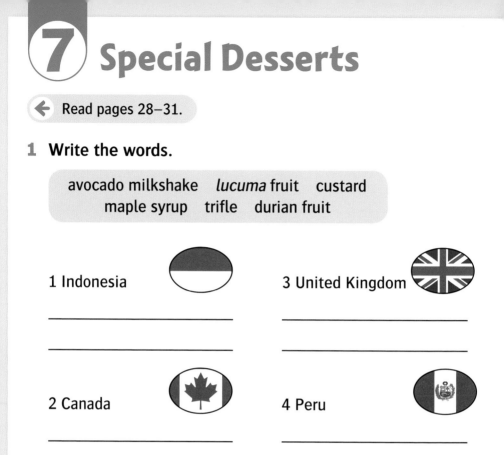

1 Indonesia

_____

_____

2 Canada

_____

3 United Kingdom

_____

_____

4 Peru

_____

2 Circle the correct words.

1 Maple syrup comes from the **sap** / **fruit** of maple trees.

2 *Alpokat* is a mikshake made with **avocados** / **durian**s.

3 *Lucuma* fruit is **orange** / **green** on the inside.

4 Custard is a traditional British **pudding** / **cake**.

5 *Mazamorra morada* is dark **green** / **purple**.

6 Durians have a very **nutty** / **strong** smell.

3 Complete the sentences.

cream   ice cream   corn   cake   buckets   chocolate

1 In Canada people collect maple sap in _____ .

2 Trifle is made with _____ , custard, fruit, and jelly.

3 *Alpokat* is made with avocados and _____ milk.

4 *Mazamorra morada* is made with purple _____ .

5 Some British people like _____ on their trifle.

6 In Indonesia people use durians to make _____ .

4 Answer the questions.

1 When do people collect maple sap?

_____

2 Why can't you eat durians on public transportation?

_____

3 What are the main ingredients of custard?

_____

4 What flavor does *lucuma* fruit have?

_____

5 What can you see on Canada's national flag?

_____

6 What dessert do you like, and why?

_____

_____

8 Giving Thanks

← Read pages 32–35.

1 Write the countries.

1 *Baisakhi* _____   3 Thanksgiving Day _____

2 *Chuseok* _____   4 *Homowo* _____

2 Write the words.

curry   turkey   yams   lentils   rice cakes   pumpkin pie

1 _____
2 _____
3 _____
4 _____
5 _____
6 _____

3 Circle the correct words.

1 People eat lots of **yams** / **rice** during *Homowo*.

2 *Chuseok* is a harvest festival in **Ghana** / **Korea**.

3 Most people eat **turkey** / **fish** on Thanksgiving Day.

4 Korean **men** / **women** do a special dance for *Chuseok*.

5 A popular Thanksgiving dessert is **cranberry** / **pumpkin** pie.

6 The Indian harvest season starts in **April** / **July**.

4 **Complete the sentences.**

ancestors   parades   temples   pie   crop   games

1 People in Ghana give the best yams to their _____ .

2 There are often street _____ during *Baisakhi*.

3 Koreans play traditional _____ during *Chuseok*.

4 Pumpkin _____ is a typical Thanksgiving dessert.

5 People visit _____ on the morning of *Baisakhi*.

6 Yams are a very important _____ in Ghana.

5 **Answer the questions.**

1 What are *songpyeon* filled with?

_____

2 When is Thanksgiving Day in the USA?

_____

3 Where do Koreans go on the morning of *Chuseok*?

_____

4 What do people in Ghana wear during *Homowo*?

_____

5 What do people watch on Thanksgiving Day?

_____

6 **Write about a festival in your country.**

_____

_____

_____

A New Restaurant

1 Imagine you are going to open a new restaurant.

2 Read the questions and make notes.

Are you going to make a lunch or dinner menu?

_____

Are you going to serve dishes from one country or many countries?

_____

Are you going to serve dishes with meat or fish?

_____

What kind of grains are you going to serve?

_____

Are there going to be any special drinks on your menu?

_____

Are you going to offer any special desserts?

_____

3 Choose a name for your restaurant and then design your menu. Decorate your menu with drawings or photographs.

4 Display your menu.

Project 2 A Festival Poster

1 Choose a food festival. It can be a food festival in your own country or in another country.

2 Complete the diagram with information about your food festival.

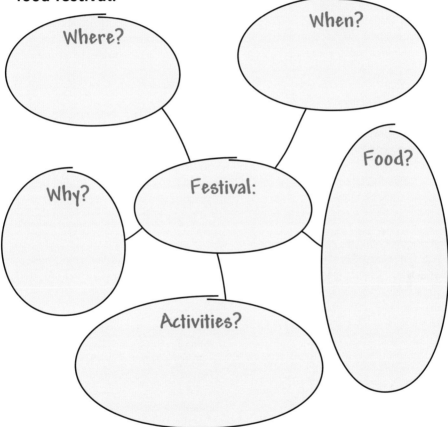

Where?

When?

Food?

Why?

Festival:

Activities?

3 Make a poster for your festival. Include the information from your diagram. Draw or paste pictures to decorate your poster.

4 Display your poster.

Glossary

ancestor someone in your family who lived a long time ago

archaeologist someone who studies history, by looking at ancient objects

artificial not real or natural

bean the seed or seed pod of a climbing plant that we eat as a vegetable

berry (*plural* **berries**) a small fruit that grows on bushes or trees

blender a machine for mixing liquids and soft foods like fruits or vegetables

blood the red liquid in your body

bone the hard part of your body that forms your skeleton

bright strong and easy to see (for colors)

broccoli a vegetable with many large green or purple flower heads

cabbage a vegetable with large, green leaves

cart a small, light box with wheels that you push or pull, often by hand

cemetery a place outside, where we put the bodies of dead people in tombs

cherry (*plural* **cherries**) a small, round red fruit with a large seed

chili pepper a small, green or red vegetable which gives a hot, spicy taste

coast the land beside the sea or ocean

coconut a large fruit with milky juice that we can drink

corn a plant that is grown for its grain, also called maize

crop a plant that we grow in large quantities

crush to break by pressing or squeezing hard

curry a dish with hot spices, often eaten with rice

customer someone who buys something

dairy product milk, and foods made from milk

delicate not strong, easy to break

dessert a sweet food

diet what you usually eat and drink

dig to make a hole in the ground

digest you do this when you eat food and your body uses it

disease a medical problem that makes you very sick

energy we need energy to move and grow, and machines need energy to work

explorer a person who travels to new places to discover new things

field an area of land where we grow crops or keep animals

fingernail the thin, hard layer on the end of your finger

fire this is produced when something burns; it's very hot

fresh not old (for food)

garlic a vegetable with a very strong smell and taste; it breaks into small parts

gelatine it's used in cooking to make a liquid thick

grain the small, hard seeds of food plants like wheat or rice

grow to get bigger

harvest the time of year when crops are ready

healthy not sick

hole a space in something

industry the production of things, especially from factories

ingredient one of the foods used to make a dish

irrigation system an artificial way of watering crops

joke something you say or do that is funny

lay eggs to produce eggs (birds, insects, and fish do this)

lentil a small, round pulse that can be green, orange, or brown

mango a tropical fruit that is yellow or red on the outside and orange on the inside

meal when people sit down and eat food

melon a large fruit with green, yellow, or orange skin

metal a hard material made from minerals

muscle a part of your body that you contract or relax to move your bones

natural something that comes from nature; it's not made by people

net it's made of string or wire; it's used to catch fish

nutrient something that we get from food to live and grow

oil a fatty liquid that we use for cooking; it comes from plants or animals

onion a round vegetable with many thin layers and a strong smell; people cry when they cut it

pan a container used for cooking; it's often made of metal

parade a public celebration in the streets

paste a soft, wet mixture

pasture an area of land covered with grass; animals feed on it

peach a round, soft fruit with red and yellow skin

pick to take flowers or fruit from the plant or tree where they are growing

pineapple a tropical fruit that is hard and rough outside and yellow inside

plow (or **plough**) to dig a field or land

pod a long, thin case with seeds inside

pond a small area of water

port a place where ships arrive and leave from

prawn a small water animal with ten legs; it turns pink when it's cooked

produce to grow or make something

protect to keep safe from danger

pulp the soft, inside part of some fruits and vegetables

pulses the seeds of some plants that we can eat, for example, lentils and beans

pumpkin a large, round vegetable with thick, orange skin

raise to feed and take care of animals

raisin a dried grape

recipe it tells you how to cook a dish

refreshing when it makes you feel less hot or less tired

respect something you feel for somebody you admire

sap the liquid in a plant or tree

sauce a thick liquid that you eat with food

savory (or **savoury**) having a taste that is salty, not sweet

seafood sea animals that we can eat, for example, fish and prawns

seed the small, hard part of a plant; a new plant can grow from this

seedling a small, young plant that grows from a seed

shellfish an animal with a shell that lives in water

skin a thin layer that covers the outside of an animal or a plant

sour having a taste like a lemon or a fruit that is not ready to eat

source where something comes from

sow to plant seeds

spice seeds or powder from plants that we use to give taste to food

spinach a dark green vegetable with big leaves

squeeze to press and get liquid out of something

stall a table or a small shop with an open front where people sell things

store to keep something to use later

temperature how hot or cold something is

temple a religious building

thick not thin

tomb the place where we put the body of a dead person

turkey a large bird that that we can eat

vegetable a plant or part of a plant that we eat as food

vendor a person who sells things, usually in the street

yard an area outside, usually with a wall

Oxford Read and Discover

Series Editor: Hazel Geatches • CLIL Adviser: John Clegg

Oxford Read and Discover graded readers are at six levels, for students from age 6 and older. They cover many topics within three subject areas, and support English across the curriculum, or Content and Language Integrated Learning (CLIL).

Available for each reader:
• Audio Pack
• Activity Book

Available for selected readers:
• e-Books

Teaching notes & CLIL guidance: **www.oup.com/elt/teacher/readanddiscover**

Subject Area / Level	The World of Science & Technology	The Natural World	The World of Arts & Social Studies
1 300 headwords	• Eyes • Fruit • Trees • Wheels	• At the Beach • In the Sky • Wild Cats • Young Animals	• Art • Schools
2 450 headwords	• Electricity • Plastic • Sunny and Rainy • Your Body	• Camouflage • Earth • Farms • In the Mountains	• Cities • Jobs
3 600 headwords	• How We Make Products • Sound and Music • Super Structures • Your Five Senses	• Amazing Minibeasts • Animals in the Air • Life in Rainforests • Wonderful Water	• Festivals Around the World • Free Time Around the World
4 750 headwords	• All About Plants • How to Stay Healthy • Machines Then and Now • Why We Recycle	• All About Desert Life • All About Ocean Life • Animals at Night • Incredible Earth	• Animals in Art • Wonders of the Past
5 900 headwords	• Materials to Products • Medicine Then and Now • Transportation Then and Now • Wild Weather	• All About Islands • Animal Life Cycles • Exploring Our World • Great Migrations	• Homes Around the World • Our World in Art
6 1,050 headwords	• Cells and Microbes • Clothes Then and Now • Incredible Energy • Your Amazing Body	• All About Space • Caring for Our Planet • Earth Then and Now • Wonderful Ecosystems	• Food Around the World • Helping Around the World